JIM HENDERSON'S
HOME COUNTRY

JIM HENDERSON'S
HOME COUNTRY

Illustrations by
Betty Brownie

Grantham House

New Zealand

Also by Jim Henderson

Gunner Inglorious (April 1945)
RMT (Official New Zealand War History, 1954)
Tobacco Farm (1954)
Te Kao 75 (1957)
22 Battalion (Official New Zealand War History, 1958)
One Foot at the Pole (1962)
Unofficial History (1964)
Open Country (1965, and five succeeding Open Country books, 1967, 1969, 1971, 1974,1982)
New Zealand's South Island in Colour (with K. & J. Bigwood, 1966)
The New Zealanders (with J. Siers, 1975)
Swagger Country (1976)
Soldier Country (1978)
The Exiles of Asbestos Cottage (1981)
Down from Marble Mountain (1983)
No Honour, No Glory (with Spence Edge, 1983)
Tales of the Coast (1984)
Jim Henderson's People (1986)
Jim Henderson's New Zealand (1989)

Also by Betty Brownlie with Ronald Lockley
The Secrets of Natural New Zealand (1987)

First published 1990

GRANTHAM HOUSE PUBLISHING

P.O. Box 17–256
Wellington 5
New Zealand

© Text 1990 Jim Henderson
illustrations 1990 Betty Brownie

ISBN 1 86934 024 8

Edited by Anna Rogers
Typeset by Setrite Typesetters, Hong Kong
Designed by Bookprint Consultants Limited, Wellington
Printed by Kings Time Printing Press of Hong Kong in association with Bookprint Consultants Limited, Wellington

Contents

CHAPTER ONE

Birds, Beasts An' Fishes Corner

WE stole a kea once, Recy Winn of Christchurch re-members. It had been trapped and taken to an Otago town as a novel pet for children who stared at it for a week, then forgot it. We were staying next door and it worried us to see a kea in an ordinary parrot cage. Its eyes haunted us. They didn't look at anyone or anything but always at far-off, remembered places.

At deepest owl-time we slunk into the orchard and stole the kea, cage and all.

Then, on returning north to the Canterbury hills, the day of days for him. We opened the door and stood back. The kea looked suspicious. He remained at the back of the cage and stared up to a high shingle hilltop. Then he grew excited and danced about until he almost fell out of the door.

He lifted his wings but didn't fly. He stood for a few minutes. He was thinking. He turned a stone over and wiped his beak on a snowberry plant, then he hopped up on to a rock and preened his feathers. He seemed to feel that the cage was still about him but that the view had improved.

Several times he raised his wings and dropped them. Perhaps they'd grown weak. I offered a grape on the end of a stick and he took it in an absent-minded way.

We decided to leave him and started to scramble down over the rocks. He hopped down and followed. 'Hey!' I said. 'You're a wild bird, remember?'

My handkerchief dropped and the kea made a clumsy dash and grabbed it and went up and away.

'Decent of him to wave goodbye,' said my fellow thief and we watched until olive green was lost against the bush-line.

A friend returned the cage secretly. May it never hold another kea.

HOW frail and thin, our link with birds with all the bubbling emotion behind their song, the beauty and glow of their colour, flight, their snug devotion of nesting.
Now George Henry McMahon of Takapuna sings.
When Riroriro Sang
Where were you when the grey warbler sang?
Up behind Bald Spur where we used to hang
On the rata vines under the great trees and hear
From the dark green valleys: the riroriro, sad and sweet and clear.

And we heard when the hills rang again and again,
A hundred echoing whistles from the speeding train
Bound for Taneatua, blow blow blow blow blow from Waihou:
And the riroriro sang: as it did a hundred years ago.

It trilled clear when the tramlines and water-chutes
Cut through the bush and a thousand great toots

Bled as man showed his disdain for their bleeding:
And the riroriro sang: unheeded and mourning and
pleading.

And it sang when men tore out the guts of the hill
From the old Tui mine: they are dammed up there still
Poisoned and dead, ready to spill when the earth starts to
shake
And the riroriro calls for the rain: and the dam starts to
break.

Will you care when the dam takes its slide and the river
No longer the giver of life, its waters the colour of liver
Writhes with the throes of the eels and the fish
And the riroriro echoes shrill through the rain: our own
death wish.

BIRDS Beasts an' Fishes Corner was a big generous
bend, with a glory-box view away out to Motueka,
about a couple of miles below Kairuru. Here's how.

The legendary Tinny Solly, driver − no, *conductor*, an
artist to his fingertips! − of Newman's red service car to
Takaka, was reaching for the last cigarette in his yellow
Three Castles packet. He flung the empty packet out into
the watertable of the wide bend.

Did it hold a priceless 'Birds Beasts and Fishes' cigarette
card, one of 50 unimaginable natural treasures and wonders
around the world? Too shy this day, I didn't ask him. And
in misery, in summer heat and over rough road stones, I
slogged down those two miles.

The packet was empty not a feather, a hair, or a scale.

'Where have you been?' asked Mum eventually.

'Nothing. Just messing about.'

But for all the empty pack, for all the absence of a Bird of Paradise, a Great Barrier Reef Fish, a terrifying formidable Great Anteater or Hippo, it became, and remains, 'The Birds, Beasts an' Fishes Corner'.

And, of course, in the mysterious ways of writing, evolves 65 years later into this chapter...

THE scene, the immaculate, delicious bakery-kitchen at Mount Crawford prison, high above a Wellington ridge, and there baker-cook Colin, beside him a beautiful blue budgerigar enjoying a stroll.

'Why doesn't he fly away, Colin?'

A wry twist of a lip from Colin. 'They clipped his wings, too.'

HE loved his aviary, a lavish collection of canaries at his home in Christchurch. Always, without fail, they burst into loving song at his return up the path after work in the evening.

Our bird lover was transferred, from the Post Office I think, over the Southern Alps to work in Westland. But one evening, to the family's joy, ending the long unaccustomed semi-silence, all of the birds burst into full-throated beautiful singing.

'Trevor's come home!' they exclaimed, hurrying out and down the path, but strangely, and rather sadly, nobody was there.

Next day a telegram arrived saying he had died in the Black Plague of the influenza epidemic, November 1918, exactly at the time his faraway canaries resumed their welcome choir.

A bush hawk fell in love with the alarm clock in Arthur Davis's bushwhackers' tent, Papanui Junction...

'No good will come of it,' said the younger bushman forebodingly. 'You might as well take the gun out and shoot the thing.'

11

The elder bushman fulled his pipe deliberately before answering. 'I reckon it's doing no harm,' he said finally. 'We'll just leave it be.'

And that is what they did, the writer Arthur Davis and his brother, bushwhacking at Papanui Junction. They first noticed the hawk when they came home from work early to grind their axes. It was sitting in the setting sun at the back of the tent. It flew off as they approached. The elder raked up embers from the banked-up fire and hung the billy on the wire hook. They would have a mug of tea before they started on the grindstone. They always did.

'Reckon it came for the scraps,' said the younger. The other didn't answer. There was no need. Of course it came for the scraps. Why else would it come?

As they sipped their scalding tea there was a rush of wings and the hawk landed again at the back of the tent and hopped over to the exact position it was in when they arrived, its shadow clearly outlined upon the calico.

'Must be warm there,' said the elder.

Then as they watched they noticed there was something queer about the bird. Its shoulders were humped and its wing-tips pointed straight down. And all the time its head moved from side to side and its feet stomped in curious regular rhythm. Both the bushmen were nonplussed. Although they had lived all their lives close to nature neither had seen anything like it.

They racked their brains for a reason.

'St Vitus' Dance?' suggested the younger.

The elder thought deeply upon it. 'Couldn't fly straight,' he replied.

They finished their tea in silence. Then suddenly the elder's face lit up. 'The clock!' he said. 'The blasted thing is listening to the alarm clock.'

The younger was doubtful. 'We'll soon see,' he said.

He moved quietly over and shifted the clock to the other side of the tent and sure enough the shadow followed and resumed its rhythmic tramping. And so there it was. They had a hawk that jived to the music of an alarm clock.

They didn't tell anybody. There was nobody to tell. They wouldn't see the cowboy from the station until the end of the week by which time the job would be cut out and they would strike camp and take their gear in on the packhorse he would bring with him. So every day they went to work and every evening the hawk homed in for his session with the clock. They grew quite attached to him and never forgot to leave some pieces of meat out for his supper. Finally, when the job was finished, they pulled the camp down and packed their gear in readiness for the packhorse. They thought of the hawk.

'Pity we couldn't have taught him to wind the clock. We could have left it with him,' suggested the younger.

THE murmurations of starlings ... how on target, this word, and lifetime admiration for this cheerful school-boy-polished-face cherub of a bird, and its sprawling unmade beds within dusty empty corrugated corners, hinting of mysteries and mice. Eggs, softly sky–tinted, indicate inheriting flights with bursts of song to come.

May I hand in hand take you to Jack Drummond's hill-top verandah, I a kid staying at Pukerunga there for two weeks while my beloved Dad died, painfully, with double pneumonia, every breath creaking. He withdrew the company I was waiting to fuse into a lifetime love, his brown eyes went out, he died.

And for the two weeks' separation up the hill from Drummond's verandah, the starlings sang on glistening and glossy, their throats gulping, eager with the excitement of a new day. Spilling over with life and its promise. I'd moon away much of the time between the singers and a book, during that time of parole, wondering without knowing, sprawled on the old bleached sofa there. A few criminal shots, oh shame, with a .22 rifle across to their 8 or 9 a.m. concerts on the dead standing trees, like quitted cicada cases, over the hill road. The scattered forest, surrendered sentinels of dead trees marking time.

I try to write for those singers in lasting thanks, but it

becomes mechanical, comes to a dutiful stop, like still
hands on piano keys. And please, Mrs Drummond, can I
have one more great Belgian biscuit of yours and another
with hundreds and thousands on its top, too?

And a nurse had come with a folded white tablecloth
over her head to help nurse Dad in the big shadowy bed on
our farmhouse down the road. By our verandah stiff fan
palms rattled.

And at night the soft green glow of the pump-up table
lamp, and wondering, dumb, was Dad really getting better
as the grownups 'hoped to say' ... because it was all so
purposefully vague until...

But the kids-time starlings there, then, remain planted,

glowing, until my own dried cicada case time comes, and I want to say I thank you for 'for singing Dad out and away', and I'm sorry about the shots, and I think I missed every-time anyhow.

M Y young nephew Michael Henderson tells of his encounter on the farm.

Alone in our only patch of tussock far back in the hills, I was full of awareness. It was so quiet, and the solitude seemed to be something that I could touch. Suddenly there was a flash of feathers, a screech, and I was ducking my head in astonishment, laughing.

The bird careered over me and circled high back over my right shoulder. I thought, still blissfully clinging to the associations of solitude, that it had probably suffered a bigger surprise than me. Not so. Down it came again, faster and lower, screeching an unearthly rasping scream, perhaps like the scream of a dive-bomber. This time I had to fling myself to the ground, all visions of a tangible solitude shattered.

After a bit I stood up, rubbing dirt off my rifle barrel. But the bird, two-thirds the size of a seagull, was coming in again. Fast and low between the fire–blackened stumps it came at me. Alarmed, I flung a rock at it. On it came, growing like a cricket ball lifting fast, sharp and true off the pitch. Batless, I hit the ground again. My back felt cringingly nude. I remember thinking how infinitely significant each crumb of dirt must be to a soldier under fire as he lies hugging the ground. But my position was ludicrous.

Apparently satisfied after several more swooping dives, the sparrowhawk flew and perched on a dead tree in the bush. I hesitated to shoot it, still not knowing what it was. Had I known, it would have made no difference. How

could I have shot such a proud, defiant little bundle of feathers, such a spirited ball of contemptuous daring? And so I hurled some stones at it, very close. It didn't shuffle an inch. Seeing the sharpness of the stones, I left my first sparrowhawk and pushed away through the pale green tussock.

A sympathetic hen proved a Godsend to one badly fed and meanly accommodated shearer on a North Canterbury farm. The narrator, for sure the redoubtable Henry Fox Chaffey of my *The Exiles of Asbestos Cottage*, enjoyed telling how an Aussie in the gang always beat him by a few Merinos and Romneys in his daily tally. Chaffey, lump it or leave it in those inelegant days, had to sleep in a hayloft. A comprehending hen daily laid an egg right beside him.

'This daily egg,' pronounced Chaffey, 'after a week managed to give me just the extra nourishment and strength to beat that Australian shearer.'

D EVOTED to their hens, which progressively died full of age and honour, this admirable farm family of Nelson pastures was asked by a visitor observing this collection of tottering ancients, 'Do you ever — er — eat your hens?'

'*Eat* our hens!' Enga Washbourn would relate, horror evident. 'Eat our hens! We can scarcely bear to eat our eggs!'

I yearned for this hen,during the bad times, the black times, when I was a prisoner of war in Bari camp, Southern Italy, shut up like a chook myself. Never believe anyone who glibly says that any living creature is better off, better fed and treated, when confined, imprisoned. Hamlet, imprisoned in a walnut, king of infinite space, would be 'troubled by bad dreams.'

Would I ever feed again, came that peasant-yearning in that place of barbed wire and bare trampled earth, that little brown hen, back home in the hills? The little half-bantam with the beautiful bobbing ruby-red comb, she ate wheat out of my hand with such trusting delicacy...

IN the tussock at Fairlie a party was shooting wallabies. One chap, posing as if a Mighty Hunter for a photo with a trophy, draped the little animal in his blazer, and grinned at the camera. The grin disappeared instantly when the wallaby, merely stunned, abruptly took off for the hills, £20 in currency notes in the lamenting chap's blazer pocket.

I'M sure Maurice Flahive told me this, how cobbers pig-hunting, maybe inland from Opotiki, spotted two Captain Cookers, nose to tail, walking the track across the valley. The men fired, dropped the leader dead, and were about to dispatch the second, when it stayed stone–still! Astounded, the pals crossed the valley, found pig number two motionless, mouth firmly clamped in the dead pig's tail. Blind! They'd shot his seeing-eye pig.

And, relates Maurice, just the work of a moment to sever the tail, lead the blind porker up to the Landrover and dispatch him with appreciation and compassion − the easiest pighunt on record so far!

BEAST and bird synchronised in a fleeting moment among lifetime's most treasured memories for Perrine Moncrieff, the noted naturalist and conservationist. Somewhere in the Lakes Rotoiti-Rotoroa area, marvelling, she looked through a screen of manuka to watch, then adore, an emperor stag, all unaware, drinking from the stream, the beauty and harmony suddenly apparent and included, down to the sparkle of the very drops of water gracious from his muzzle.

Then perfection, as if from a ballet movement — the stag, as though giving thanks, lifted his antlers, exactly as a native pigeon, in green and snow-white glory, flew through the very centre of the raised antlers.

A sign and omen comprehensible only to the wisest and most compassionate seers of Ancient Greece.

PIG yarns, yes! And away to that noble man Archdeacon James Young. Conducting a funeral, he was held up, delay after delay. They just wouldn't let him, and the restless grieving party, into the cemetery, the gates shut firmly.

Afterwards James, annoyed, tackled the sexton: 'Why the dickens did you keep us hanging and hanging around like that? Most annoying to all concerned.'

The sexton hung his head.

'As a matter of fact it was most awkward,' he explained miserably. 'You know, a half-grown young pig had fallen into the just–dug grave, and the terrified sobs and squeals as we tried to drag it out, would have broken up any funeral party, in disaster or farce.'

URGED to write about and to share in homage this rare concession from the kingdom of fiords and mountain, Patricia Neame of Manurewa eventually did so, choosing to write in the third person, as if, I imagine, in tribute to those other ones of creation. The summer came to Milford Sound in the year of her first trip to Fiordland.

All her young life in Auckland summer was not summer unless you went swimming; everyone in Auckland lived near a beach. She was to find that the glacier water, and the depth of that Milford water was incredibly chilling, almost painful, and her first dip was a short sharp experience.

She had heard that the Cook Strait swimmers used petroleum jelly to insulate themselves from the cold water on long endurance swims, so she took to this practice and found it worked quite well. The next step was to get by mail-order post some long woollen underwear a size too small so that it fitted skin-tight. Then she found out that Harrisons Cove (an inlet where the water was shallow near the shore) on fine days was decidedly warmer than anywhere else at Milford Sound.

In the two-and-a-half seasons she spent at Milford including a wintering over 1948, '49 and '51, never once did she feel any different about the place in all its moods, the sky, the rain, the Bowen Falls in flood so loud you heard it in your sleep; it remains spectacularly the one most beautiful place in the world.

On her first trip up the sound to Anita Bay the dolphins came. To the delight of everyone, they frolicked in wash from the bow. When visitors stopped for fishing or for taking photographs they would come up to the boat and poke their heads out looking at us as we were looking at them. One was more cheeky than the rest. She called him 'Nosey' and from the outset the light in his eye was special, and captured her imagination. She called him 'he' but was never to know if that was its sex, it never mattered anyway. She called him her Brother in the Sea, so warmly did she feel his kindred spirit. On her days off she would go with the tourists on the launch *Donald Sutherland* (so named after the explorer of the area) and they would go right up to the sound entrance,to see the fur seals bathing on the rocks, or put off people at Anita Bay to look for green-stone, a keepsake to touch and tell of in the years ahead.

Nosey became an attraction of his own. She made loops out of twigs lashed into a circle and as fast as she would toss them in the air he would jump clear of the water and catch them on his snout, returning them gleefully. Which-ever side of the boat she worked when they stopped to fish, there he would perform and then come back for the accolades.

Sometimes, instead of doing the tourist bit, she would leave the launch in a dinghy and row to Harrisons Cove for a day on her own, a day when she could swim, explore the bush, listen to the birds and relax in the sun. It was on such a day that she found she was not alone in the water.

Here, gentle in approach, was a fin. He quickly lifted his head to show a friendly eye than squeaked a muted 'hello' to her. She rolled over and over with joy at the encounter and reached out to touch him. He did not come nearer but surveyed her from five feet away. She jack-knifed, went under to see if he was alone and to get some idea of his size. He submerged too and seemed to be grinning at her

(as well he might) for in less than a minute she was up gasping for air. So they played, she embraced him and kissed him, he in turn nuzzled and smooched her with a caress as gentle as a butterfly.

In excitement he would propel himself out of the water and back-pedal with dexterity, laughing hilariously; she should bounce with the buoyancy of her body and splash with her arms to show her joy.

He would come back to her as if to say; 'Never mind, you look so silly, don't try so hard.' He let her hold his fin and climb astride him and gently he would move with her,

quick to complain if, in her clumsy way, she covered his
blowhole.

When the coldness forced her to leave the water and
wrap up warmly for a while, he would wait as close to the
shore as possible and, as if understanding the mere mortality
of her fragile skin and nerve system, he would carry on a
disappearing-reappearing game. When she thought he had
gone she had a warm drink from the thermos, packed up
the dinghy, and then he would come back and squeak at
her when she least expected it.

As she rowed back to the meeting place he kept pace
with the oar going in and out of the water, and as she found
the rowing stressful and her breathing was labouring he
would blow in rhythm with her stress. Reluctant to say
goodbye after the dinghy had been attached to the launch
and she had her feet firmly on the deck, he followed for a
while then joined the others and was lost in anonymity.

No day was ever more delightful than that first day. For
the whole season they shared a comradeship: if ever she did
not go on the launch others would tell her, he came looking
for you today. She tried to tell them all that he would play
with anyone who wasn't aftaid of him. But no − if he came
and she wasn't there he would lose interest and go away.

So it was, the bonding. It was only so because she shared
his world, believed, 'A mammal am I, a mammal is he',
and he gave that something special, her Brother in the Sea.

CURIOUS, on the hospital ship, back in southern lati-
tudes, the morning attendances and dressing done, we
war-wounded, as if in pilgrimage, would make, limp, shuffle
or cautiously plod our various ways, some with crutches, or
a stick, frozen in white plaster, or discreetly bandaged,
some helped (and some two or three to our grief blind)

instinctively, as if lured, towards the stern of the white ship with its bold Red Crosses of Mercy and civilisation. And there, silent most times for the remaining free hour or half-hour, we would watch, in adoration and worship, the distilled, effortless, kingdom-come flight of the albatross. It was from the souls of dead sailors. We watched and knew. And, at the end, may the flight of the albatross bear us gently away.

CHAPTER TWO

Women

THERE was this dear lady, elderly, who had been widowed for many years, and who had been raised in an orphanage. She began, in her late teens, to show ability at water-colours, particularly of flowers. She married and was driven into the backblocks, into the land like a post — it was not much of a farm.

After some years of her widowhood, I asked her: 'What does it all add up to? All your many, many years of marriage before he died?'

She replied: 'He never saw no beauty in nothing. A bed to sleep in and a table to sit at.'

THE two girls were great friends at boarding school but they never met properly until about 15 years later. Then the beautiful one from the city, full of high fashion, went curiously to her dear friend in the country.

After a while she enquired, 'And what, dear, do you do in your spare time?'

The reply came without hesitation: 'In my spare time, I go to the lavatory.'

UP in Northland masculine congratulations on an engagement would irritate many a merry maiden overhearing them: 'By Jove, he's lucky, he's lucky getting a girl like that for a wife. Why, she's as good as a man in the shed!'

A son and his father, who was a carpenter, were board-ing for a week in the Far North. Dad was doing a carpentry job and his son was lending a hand. Dad, a rather pontificating old coot, leaned back from the supper table one evening, when they were getting bored and said; 'Your generation! The behaviour of youth today is a shock-ing disgrace. Why,' said he 'I never even saw my wife's ankles until we were married.'

And with that, bored to the back teeth, his young son remarked tartly, 'And what happened when you did, Dad, eh? What happened then?'

MY beloved Aunt Adelaide was something of a snob, as they used to say in the old days. She felt herself 'a cut above'. Her devoted husband, called 'little Tat', worked in a bank.

Here they are in a great maze made of tall hedges, way back in the sweltering summer of 1902. They are on their honeymoon, hot as blazes, I think in Taranaki. Worn out from trudging endlessly round this wretched maze, they press on, then double back, but just can't get out.

Finally, in the boiling sun, they collapse on a bench, right in the middle of the maze.

In fury, Aunt Adelaide hurls at her husband: 'Must you say reound and reound when I'm so tired!'

YOUNG Robin said her crusty old Scots grandfather in Dunedin knew Robbie Burns and all things Scots backwards. Dunedin radio had a regular programme, *A Wee Sprig o' Heather*.

'But,' observed Robin, 'Grandfather never listens to *A Wee Sprig o' Heather unless there are visitors!*'

A young daughter's toast to herself: 'As I have to live with myself, may I always like myself.'

A veteran farm wife became irked by a prissy city visitor. Her husband, unloading a trailer, had just explained, 'I've come to spread the manure.'

'Don't say that, say "fertiliser",' said the visitor.

'For heaven's sake don't start confusing him,' snapped his wife. 'It's taken me years to get him to say "manure".'

A captive infantryman, a Christchurch chap, was there, among the suffering marchers. With Germany disintegrating, early in 1945, bands of prisoners of war under guard were marched to and fro across the countryside as the frontiers buckled. In snow and cold and slush these Kiwi prisoners, weak from long captivity and acute thirst, entered a tiny German village still burning from an air raid that day by Allied aircraft RAF and USAF bombers. An utterly innocent obscure little village, thrashed and gutted and burning. Old men and women, the rest away at the front, were dazedly pulling dead and wounded, including children, out of the wreckage, some still on fire.

'Wasser bitte, Mutter [Water, Mother]. Wasser bitte, Mutter,' cried some of the prisoners.

And, indeed, here and there a woman or two paused, to bring out a bucket of water for the prisoners, their enemies, passing by.

Infuriated, the German guards kicked over the buckets and fair enough, too. The sorely tried prisoners comprehended all right, for many had been behind barbed wire for four years, companions of close suffering. They knew they could have done the same, if this were Collingwood or Greytown or Putaruru.

'But the look of utter bewilderment on the faces of the German women, their sorrow at the guards doing this went deep into us, instantly,' the Kiwi infantryman related. He and others began to feel this was a worldwide quality among women of all nationalities; something universal had reached out and touched them.

Their unspoken sympathy and understanding, so evident, were so refreshing, perhaps even better than, water to the prisoners who, strengthened, marched on, marvelling, and wondering.

'Wasser bitte, Mutter.'

BEAUTIFUL, but alas forgetful, she was among a war-time gang of farmworkers in northern Italian fields where the occasional guards were venal and lackadasical. News had circulated of a South Pacific wartime wonder, highly coveted long red flannel or woollen Kaiapoi under-pants from occasional parcels from home. In whispered asides, she made it clear that handsome concessions would be made for a pair. This, she further emphasised, was solely due to her own mercy, because the pitifully aged grandfather she adored was in ailing health and otherwise would not last another winter.

The Kiwi prisoner of war, in a daze of trading and anti-cipation round the prison camp, got a pair. The clothing handed over, a judicious week later, in an inconspicuous hole in a haystack, the exchange began to be honoured.

Judge the Kiwi's astonishment and churn of emotion when, suddenly taken aback, he found the lovely one's shanks sheathed in grandpa's promised pink pants!

A terrible ache, akin to stitch, set in as he strove in vain to supress mirth, but his muffled chuckles mounted into roars of laughter blending into hysteria, which seldom goes with amorous intent, culminating in her mystification, be-wilderment, then rage. Thoroughly nettled, she gathered herself together and bolted, never to venture near him again.

'I still sigh over it, so near yet so far,' says he half a century later, 'but then I can't help busting into laughing full bore myself too!'

SHE would come every week, this Italian girl, and put flowers on the raw and lonely grave of a German soldier, by Cassino, a Milton man noted.

Cassino was a terrible place. It grinned at us like a

smashed, decayed old mouth. It left its mark on soldiers.

Every time she came along with the flowers the boys would be at it again, sharply divided. Some reckoned she should be booted out of it.

'Give the bitch a bullet,' one chap said once, suddenly, a good chap too. Whether he meant it or not I don't know.

Others said: 'Good on her. At least here's one Ite with the guts to show her real feelings. And after all, he's dead, isn't he, and gee — just look around how many of us would ever get someone doing that to our grave?'

THE railcar stops in savage country, furious stunted manuka somewhere near Cronadun, a wilderness. A woman gets off to be followed by a sullen man, wordless, expressionless, to ride ahead of her on a bicycle. She trudges behind, about 40, old grey hunched coat, faded dress, shoulders bent, face slumped with wrinkles — she'd done, had it, she'd been beaten — but hang on a minute, not quite...

As she trudges away, suddenly I glimpse something and change my mind. I see her shoes, new shoes, red shoes — brave shoes. The last touch of defiance. No. She's not done — yet.

OH yes, she had a great job — at least it was a job anyhow, on a pig farm, and regularly (I think it was daily?) she had to see to a barrow-load of pig manure, wheel it to the place they dumped it, whereupon a loathsome curtain of disturbed rats never failed to shin up the wall and briefly vanish. They seemed impervious to poisons and traps. Reasonably enough, all this was beginning to get her down.

Salvation came in the farm's horizon setting of mountains, for, like a saviour searchlight, into her mind came: the psalm, 'I will lift up mine eyes unto the hills, from which cometh my help'. After that, she reckoned, around the tipping time, she'd look up 'and it was okay'.

THIS teenage girl was simpering and whimpering after reading some romantic tale; she was aching for orchids. Mother, overhearing the whimpering, advised: 'Dear, please realise, you live in New Zealand. We're New Zealanders. You'll be damned lucky if ever you land up with a bunch of silverbeet!'

A wooden box nailed to the wall of the milking shed seemed to symbolise the times. Over the years, a cavalcade of mothers pushing their babies in battered cane prams across the paddock to the milking shed, umbrella or oilskin protecting the little ones against rain. From pram poked into a corner of the separator room, they graduated later to the wall box, parked there daily for five hours altogether — two-and-a-half hours each shift. And so on, until a succession of babysitters was bred up.

The poor little mite — no wonder why wide-eyed — from the silence of eternity launched into the slap of belts, the chug of the vacuum pump, the whine of the separator, the suck and slurp of the releaser.

The dawn patrols, the yawning eye-rubbing kids at school, pupils and teachers not giving a damn, the skin with that certain sheen and the whispering Shylock smell of milk?

No women and child labour in New Zealand — appalling! Only the foundation, unacknowledged of course, of our mighty dairy industry.

HE wandered out into the kitchen looking irritatingly for draughts in all directions, slamming windows, probing, checking with a thin whine.

'You'd better put the plug in the sink while you're at it,' quoth the youngest daughter. A superb example of Kiwi laconic humour, but they called it 'cheek' in those days.

SAILING the world alone, *Sheila in the Wind* author Adrian Hayter recalled that every nationality he met had two questions. Women: 'Were you lonely?' And men: 'Were you afraid?'

WHAT child do you like the most?' I asked, a curly one.

'The one who is sick, or the one who is away,' came her admirable answer.

THE Reverend Ormond Burton MC was a magnificent man, verging on sainthood; from many trials he triumphed in his gentle spirit. One day a woman, among a group of us visiting him and his dear wife, said, 'You know, the Reverend Burton, he actually gave away in winter, in a freezing winter, his only overcoat.'

Mr Burton smiled and nodded, agreeing with the woman. Later I reminded Mrs Burton of this and she, too, gave a sweet smile and said, with the gentlest of expressions, 'Yes, it is true, he did give away his only overcoat, and, incidentally, for the following fortnight I had to look after him when he went down with influenza.'

CHAPTER THREE

Men

BEWILDERMENT, notes Mary Rakich of Kaitaia, up Ahipara way at the gumfield toilings, when a Yugoslav worker recently arrived was asked what he was having for lunch.

'Hawk sandwiches,' replied the immigrant cheerfully.

Growing perplexity, until somone probed further, to be told: 'Why, hedgehawk hedgehop sandwiches.'

Must try it myself one day — the gypsies pronounced them quite delicious.

DAD'S own army, Westland version. A sudden Air Raid Precautions rally and rehearsal, the self-reliant miners well to the fore, and among the scattered assumed 'casualties and wounded' was Wattie, an alleged 'spinal injury', strapped firmly to a board and tied up, no movement possible to jar broken bones. The first aid men considerately put him in a hollow out of any wind in the Stillwater slaughteryards — and forgot him. Manoeuvres long over, not until 9.30 p.m. guiltily remembering in the pub, did they set out.

Truly torrential rain had been falling for hours. Wattie was unbelievably saturated, what a sight, the hollow nearing drowning level too.

I hopped over the fence to Karl Marx Villa, Onekaka, to take down on tape the words of medical man Dick Moth: 'Wattie expressed his dissatisfaction.

'He cursed the war, the Japs, the Patriotic Effort, the Forces, he didn't care where they were fighting, he wasn't interested anymore in self-preservation. *Did he go hostile! He wouldn't even drink with us when we got him back to the pub.* He dissociated himself from us entirely, he wanted no more of us, he wouldn't attend any more St John Ambulance meetings, he couldn't have cared less about our ARP efforts.

'We felt − er − a lttle bit guilty, poor old Wattie − but aw − these things happen in a war, don't they?'

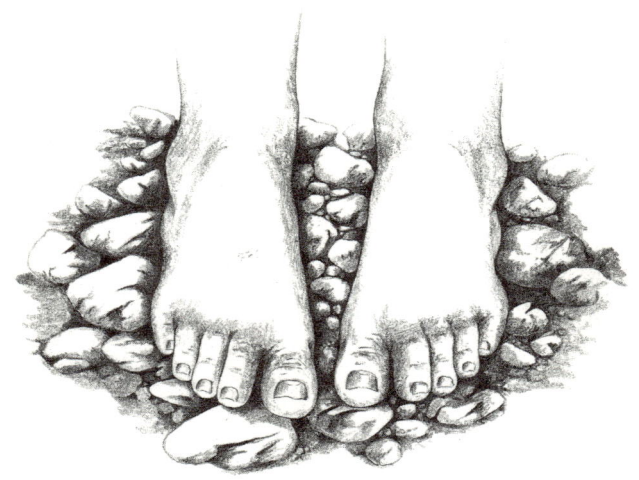

WRY Alan Brown used to relate how his old father continuously recalled the hardships of his schooldays. The road to school grew progressively longer and longer, the snow got deeper and deeper, while the flints on the road became harder and harder on his bare feet. His attire became more woefully ragged over the years of recollection, until one day in super exaggeration, he shouted as a finale: 'Glad of a crust!'

Musingly, Alan, admirable apple farmer of Mapua, commented: 'Listening to the old man in full fig, I'm positive Dad had confused his childhood lifestyle completely with Napoleon's retreat from Moscow.'

A talented gentleman from Oamaru, his name alas temporarily faded, enjoyed recalling the leathery old drover showing off his dexterity with his stockwhip before a wayside car of tourists.

'Show us how it works! Go on, be a sport!'

'Right — stand by.'

'SNAP!' and a poor labouring fieldmouse was no more, now in heaven.

'Do it again!' and ditto for a luckless lizard sunning itself on a stone.

'Great! Hey, get that bee sitting on that post.'

'No fear, not bees,' warned the drover, probably once a trade unionist, 'they're organised.'

A S my two mates and I, recalls Len Wilson, sweated across the Dart Flats in the summer of 1951—52 under our 90-pound packs, we encountered Bill Barrowman splitting red beech posts. His axe strokes were so relaxed and accurate they nearly looked lazy. Tall, shy, short black hair sprouting in all directions, he invited us over to the hut on the bush edge for a cup of tea. I noticed that he was very thin and though he moved with cat-like ease over uneven ground, he remained a little hunched. His hospitable wife promptly filled us with those trembling tender scones straight from the oven. Bill rarely uttered: She rushed on at the rate of Aunt Daisy.

Ranging for two months over those tumbling valleys and blistering tops stretching right over to the Hollyford — we were set on making a fortune from deerskins — we emerged three or four times for supplies and of course saw more of the Barrowmans. Between Bill's own reluctant accounts of his exploits and the highly articulate stories told by Hugh Miller, the Bermudan at Paradise, we developed a respect amounting to awe.

In the Depression Bill had tramped for a week up the Whataroa carrying a great load of old fire hose for the sluicing claim he had prospected. His camp, 60 feet above river level, was washed out in a flood. He had pioneered that culling on the Main Divide; he had an 8000-footer named after him, having clambered up it with gear I would guess was no more sophisticated than Arawata Bill's.

Then came the war. Volunteer or conscript I don't know — probably volunteer as he was camped under canvas — he contracted chest trouble, reported sick, was quickly dispatched as a malingerer. Pleurisy and TB followed, but for the rest of his working life he followed the back country skills, such as post splitting, that were still open to him.

I think he must have loved living right there in view of Mount Earnslaw, for twenty years later I found him and Mrs Barrowman retired to an old cottage just out of Glenorchy. The old grin would still light up but it was fairly plain from his breathing and the tell-tale flush that he wouldn't, as my mother says, make old bones. He didn't.

THIS chap came to help in a paddock at Tauhoe, grubbing thistles and rushes, the entire conversation consisting of him glancing up at the sky and saying, 'There's a big 'awk.'

About an hour later: 'There's another big 'awk.'

And that was that, the total conversation of the day. 'And quite enough', some Kiwis will agree.

SPARTAN, the process of paying a compliment to a woman around 1911. The Barrows Brothers — Harry, Dave and Ern — bewhiskered, peerless bushwhackers, black singleted, in long red flannel underpants, handling their gleaming axes with the pride of crusader knights, now sitting in the family kitchen, in the agony and embarrassment of attempting to give Mary a little gift. Mary's husband, George Mearing, the rouseabout, fresh and undismayed from England, revived the scene.

The three Barrows, in the kitchen, are seated in line on the old wooden form. Ern pulls out a picture postcard, somewhat of a novelty then, and all brothers examine it, in turn, tilting it in their hands, and then silently and solemnly returning it to Ern. He thrusts out the card to Mary.

45

'Here. You like it?'

'Oh, pretty.'

'Well, keep it then.'

Ah well, back to the Round Hill whare of slabs and split-sack bunks, the camp oven of native pigeon, spuds and pumpkin, dead man's arm, cockies' joy (treacle) on morning toast, the stars to brood on briefly at the doorway, and the dreams the pubkeepers clawed down of a lttle farm of your very own one day ...someday...

A turn about with vengeance recorded by 30977 Hastings. During Lord Freyberg's inaugural tour of New Zealnad as Governor-General, about two hours' drive from the town where he was due for a mid-morning civic reception, the vice-regal car, pendant fluttering, drove onto one of those one-way bridges that distinguish South Island main highways from modern roads. simultaneously, a battered truck drove on at the other end.

The vehicles halted, face to face, and the vice-regal chauffeur sounded his horn imperiously. But the truck stayed put, its load of empty cream cans dancing a noisy jig to the tune of the ancient motor. Next the aide-de-camp jumped out to deliver crisp lecture on *lese-majeste*.

The truck driver, rolling a cigarette, cut him short. 'Listen,' he said. 'I took orders from Tiny for five bloody years and I'm not taking any more.'

Whereupon the gracious representative of His Gracious Majesty, who had heard and understood, gave an unaccustomed order. Smilingly Freyberg signalled his worried aide to retreat.

WET boot men are a special breed, with special hearts and souls. 'In twenty years of rangering and many, many trips, I never went up there once without being spiritually uplifted,' wrote, when I specially asked, a wet boot man I love, Max Polglaze, custodian of the Mount Arthur-Table-lands country 1969-88. Then, what a loss, he quit stifled, overwhelmed by management prescriptions.' Sad; I asked for a special fragment, with love. He wrote: 'Here, on these tablelands, listen especially to the silence. Remote from the sounds of man, remote from the voice of rivers, the only sound is of wind in tussock, or here and there the tinkle of a creek, or a solitary skylark warbling on high. And in the quietness of calm, when the wind is still... nothing — absolute quiet, a beautiful silence.'

'OH, strike, how did you get that wonderful line of yours in *Sings Harry*: "And the river running down?"' I asked Denis Glover at Onekaka. 'It always moves me, deeply.'

'Where the hell,' replied the poet, 'do you expect a bloody river to run?'

'SPLENDID job for a wet day,' said the boss. 'All those spuds we dug and stacked in the shed, sort 'em out, eh, into big ones to sell to the fussy old coot at the store, then spuds for the house, pig spuds, and useless or rotten ones.'

His farmhand was back in an hour. 'No good boss. No good. Have to make too many decisions.'

WHEN my wanderings end, says Waldo, now working in Auckland, I hope my front bedroom window won't be flowers, it will be the wild ocean and the rocks and the blowhole playing.

I was born just south of the Pancake Rocks where the blowholes are, and standing among all the people staring in awe, it made me realise I lived in one of the most beautiful spots of New Zealand.

I have travelled from Cape Reinga to Bluff, but you get to the Pancake Rocks and as you wander down through the little path there's little signs there telling you to beware, and when the tide surges in and you must stand back, *up comes the blowhole*.

And it's the force of the water rushing into the cave and the vent at the top under that extreme pressure that creates that big spout.

And it's my Whale of the West Coast.

CHAPTER FOUR

Grim Diggery

A ND there, the frozen battle zone around the Sangro River, Southern Italy, Christmas Eve, 1943, infantryman Mick Kenny went over to visit his brother in the Maori Battalion — and in the distance, the sound of Germans singing 'Silent Night', and then Maori Battalion joining in, harmonising. And Kenny writing later: 'I have thought more of this incident perhaps than any other, especially at Christmas when I hear the singing of carols.'

A year later Sergeant Kenny was wounded a week before Christmas, the labouring frontline bloodily approaching northern Italy, five months of war to go ... The place, Faenza, and one much-celebrated Kiwi sitting in a large shell hole half full of very cold water. The Kiwi had a short board, and was using it as a paddle. Two mystified British military police were looking down at him. The Kiwi looked up and, with a disgusted look, remarked, 'you two bastards can go to hell, I'm going home.'

And he went on paddling, old soldier 89842 of Hunterville will tell you.

H E was tall, the man who knocked at our back door that morning. One time, he must have been broadshouldered and well built, but now he was thin and stooped and his clothes, clean but shabby, hung loosely on him. He spoke in a well-modulated voice.

'Good morning, perhaps you would like to see this reference?' and he handed me a card. Surmounted by the badge of the RSA, the card said the caller was genuine and had the backing of the association.

I, Jim Forsyth, heard the man cough, a hard dry cough. I looked up from the little card, and the sight of his face shocked me, white and drawn, and high on the cheeks were two pink spots, His eyes seemed sunken and unnaturally bright. He coughed again, that racking cough I'd heard many times no need to ask what caused it.

'Where'd you pick up the gas, Dig?'

He smiled, began to reply, coughed instead, murmured 'Sorry,' then said, 'In front of Amiens, know the place?'

'Yes.' I told him my regiment and division.

We talked. He seemed to have forgotten what he'd called for. I asked what brought him to these parts. He opened a small suitcase, showed a series of writing pads with pencil attached, and told me the price was ninepence each. At that moment my wife's voice said, 'Would you care for a cup of tea?' She'd seen the poor chap was hungry.

Round the table we talked as ex-soldiers do. Gradually, he revealed that a medical board had awarded him a small pension, but that had been reduced recently. No, he wasn't married, and reading between the lines I thought there was a sad story here. Asked about selling writing pads, with pencils attached, he grinned ruefully and confessed he'd only sold one that morning. His share was threepence.

Standing at the door after he had gone I thought things over. The more I thought, the madder I became until my wife's shocked voice said, 'Jim!' I had been cursing out loud, a thing I very rarely did, and my little boy was gazing at me in bewilderment. Something told me that for one Digger in the Depression of the 1930s, the end of the road was not far off.

MAKING orange juice and taking it to the wounded soldiers around the wards was my job as an assistant steward on the hospital ship RMS *Atlantis*, tells E. Gale of Christchurch.

We pulled out of Naples after bringing British, Canadian, American and some German wounded on board, these wounded from the Anzio beach-head conflict, where the Germans inflicted many casualties on the unsuspecting Allied troops.

I was a very popular chap on this ship, I can tell you — a nice cool glass of orange after dirt-ridden water on the Italian mainland was a Godsend to our wounded. And the

German wounded wondered what I was giving them, as they'd not seen oranges for many years. They had just about forgotten them.

This, too, sticks in my mind. Making toast for the dining room was another of my duties; I'd cut the crusts off the bread and go out after breakfast to feed the ever-hungry seagulls. It was great fun to get the big gulls to dive down, right in the middle of the Mediterranean Sea, and take crusts from my hands.

One moring I noticed a captured German medical orderly looking at me in great amazement. With all the food shortages he'd been through in the war, he couldn't understand this. But of course it was either me feeding the gulls or throwing the crusts to the fish.

I motioned to the German orderly to do the same. At first he declined, but then he too saw the big gulls sweeping down to grab the crusts — it was a thrill to him.

And there we were, two enemies, feeding the gulls, the war nearly over, and we were going home with only seagulls swooping down, not Stuka dive-bombers.

A young seviceman on three days' leave, coming home in high spirits to his wife and baby daughter, breasted the hill and saw his village below. Suddenly a German plane, shot down and striving for a safe landing, skimmed the trees just above him.

'Don't let them jettison their bombs,' he prayed. 'Oh dear God, don't let them jettison.' As he broke into a run, the ground shook, he saw his village disappear into a pall of smoke and dust: the sound of a distant *crump* told him a minute later, as he reached the ruins of his home, that the plane, too, had met with disaster.

One side of the house was almost completely demolished, and it was here he found his young wife dying, her body blasted almost to shreds. He had time to lift her gently and call her name. She opened her eyes wide and tried to touch

his face, but with a sigh was gone.

Frederick, our serviceman, Frederick Parmee, poet and teacher, put her down and dazedly groped around for the baby and his mother-in-law. She he found upstairs across the bed but utterly untouched. Together they descended among the shambles to beneath the remains of the stairs and there was the baby in her pram where her mother had pushed her, dusty under all the debris but safe and screaming. Frederick took her up for a moment, then, with death in his heart, gave her to his mother-in-law and set out towards a spiral of smoke that told him where to look for the murdering plane, tears and sobs shaking him but not weakening his determination to avenge this hideous act if anyone had survived the crash landing.

It did not take long to find the smashed German machine

still burning, the pilot dead in the cockpit and the co-pilot sprawled on the grass some distance away, crushed, mutilated, but still alive, calling feebly.

Picking up a boulder, Frederick stood over the dying man, intending to crush his head in, kill him to avenge himself and his family. But as Frederick explained in a rare moment, the man was just a dying boy who had no idea of the calamity he had helped create, a boy far from home and in need of comfort. The stone fell to the ground and Frederick slid his arms carefully under the young German's shoulders.

Like most scholars, Frederick could speak the language well enough, so, bending low to the few whispered words, he learned that the lad was twenty and had a young wife whose new baby he had never seen. Pity took the place of the red rage Frederick had felt, and he followed the faint final words and removed a locket, identity disc and a diary from the crushed body.

Talking softly, he reassured over and over until the boy's breathing slowed and eventually stopped, then gently he laid him down and turned his face again to home, determined that one German wife and mother would hear how bravely her man had died.

Footnote: Frederick Parmee, author of *The Road*, *The Sounds of Now*, *Two Poems of Revolution*, a distinctive New Zealand poet of the 1970s and an innovative teacher in Whangarei and Matakana Island, in a rare moment spoke of the tragedy to fellow writer Peggy Dunstan.

THIS shows that compassion is not necessarily always within the walls of a hospital, where holding onto someone's hand helps so much — links you from that isolation, lightens the darkness.

Anyhow this was out near the battlefield, around Florence, and this act of compassion I'd like to recall here, now, and with respect to our medical people too.

This litle girl, where the chaps were having their meals, this little girl was just sitting there with her hands cupped and if anyone had some bread left when the meals were over they'd pop it into her cupped hands. Some chunks of bread which she would wrap up in the proper way, in the bag, with great appreciation, nodding and smiling. Always wrapping up these little fragments.

She had only one leg, the other, of course, had been lost recently in this struggle for freedom and democracy. And Arthur Davis came up to this girl. Wry and humorous Arthur Davis from Taihape, he was a sapper, engaged in the laying and defusing of land mines; just drifting through.

He said, 'I suppose you take the bread home, rebake and then sell it, do you?'

'Yes sir,' she said. 'Mother and I do pound it up and we do remake it but we sell it for money to buy a new leg for me.'

And, filled with great rage at this, at what one of our freedom-devoted Allied mines had done to the wee girl, he said, teeth tight, 'Right!'

And off he went and grabbed a cobber. 'Get going. We're off ' he said 'into the truck. Don't frig about.'

They drove to some depot and they swiped a 44-gallon drum of petrol and they shot off to the black market, where, undetected all the way, they sold it for a great wad of lira. The Gods were with them all the way, no red caps — nothing. They got through with it, this great wad of money. They returned and there was the little girl, sitting with her hands cupped up next day.

Arthur went up to her and then tipped out his money, shoved it all over her and it overflowed into her lap and he said, 'Right! Off you go now, bugger off and buy yourself a bloody leg.'

And then, he too, nearly started to drop into tears himself, touched — the comic soldier that he was.

I must record the brilliant medical officer in Maori Battalion. The American was drifting past and he said to the Maori sergeant, 'We've got a world-beater medico. One of our fellas lost his hand at the wrist — our medico stitched him up and he's getting back the use of his hand. He can actually use his fingers now. Brilliant!'

The Maori sergeant congratulated him. Said he was truly delighted the American's hand was working again, a fine achievement.

'But hear about my own medical officer in Maori Battalion' (and this was in the Sangro area, I believe, in Southern Italy).

'My own medical officer, he's pretty bright too. Poor Hemi, the other day he had his stomach shot out with a chunk of shrapnel and my officer didn't hesitate for a moment. He leaped clean over the stone wall, grabbed an old ewe there, ripped out his knife, removed the guts and back over and popped it in Hemi. Sewed him up! Good oh!'

With that the American staggered back in horror. 'Oh lordy of heaven, surely not! surely not! Did he live?'

'Live?' replied the sergeant 'live? He lambed a month later!'

PERFECTLY true. In another prisoner of war hospital in Italy, there were some who were dear old nuns; others were vinegary. But this dear old nun was in charge of the linen and caring for the dishing out of food, such as there was — 'splitting the atom,' we said. Anyhow, this time the Red Cross parcels were not coming through, the food had dropped away to next to nothing. A tangible gloom hung over the hospital. One depressed English soldier, half asleep leaned back in his bed, stretched his arms and yawned: 'Ah, things are f—ing grim.'

And with that, the little old nun came quietly up beside him and asked in Italian, 'What does, and then she repeated 'Things are f—ing grim,' 'What does that mean?'

And he replied in Italian, very embarrassed, stuttering and stammering, the first thing that came into his head. 'Oh, that means God bless you!'

So the first thing every morning and lastly every night, round the ward went the dear old lady, bending most graciously, hands held together, smiling her blessing and saying to us all — and did it lift our spririts — saying to as all: 'Things are f—ing grim.'

MANY years ago, writes James Lennox-King, not long after the Second World War, I fell into conversation with a stranger. I found he had been a prisoner of war in Japanese hands. The camp he was in was in Malaya, the Japanese commandant a cruel arrogant man who displayed the worst characteristics of the Japanese in uniform.

One day his behaviour had been so bad that my acquaitance, an officer of some seniority himself, shouted something to the effect of 'I wish you were a rugby ball — I would kick you so far over the wire they'd never find you again!' The commandant strode up to him, his eyes blazing; my man steeled himself for blows or being dragged off for torture. Instead, the commandant said, 'Rugby? You played rugby in New Zealand? You know Ron Bush?'

Every rugby player and follower in New Zealand knew Ron Bush, that marvellous fullback. Surprised, the Kiwi said, 'Yes, I know Ron Bush. We played for the same club — in fact we both played for the New Zealand University side in your damned country!'

The commandant's eyes opened wide. 'You did? You play against Tokyo University?' 'Yes, I did.' 'Aaaah — I captain that Tokyo University side! Ron Bush and I became good friends — he come sometimes to my home. My little boy, he seven. I teaching him play rugby, so Ron Bush gave my little boy a pair his rugby boots [holding his hands about 18 inches apart] and my little boy gave Ron Bush a pair his rugby boots. [holding his forefingers a few inches apart]. And you play in that team...! Aaaah!'

From that time the regime became human, the prisoners found the guards respectful, the whole atmosphere of the camp changed. It is good to know that a reflection of the prowess of that great footballer Ron Bush on the rugby field cound help imprisoned men so long after and so far away.

WHO cares, who, oh my lost comrades? Who to answer the eternal account? More than 6000, almost all soldiers, of the Commonwealth (not counting the 'enemy dead') are buried in the accursed hungry desert of 1941 we knew from the Egypt border reaching to near Tobruk. A carnival for ants, for cynical scarabs pushing their own little planets.

What and where our own New Zealand dead, shadowed by the Saint, from Sidi Rezegh battlefield, Libya? Our comrades from that bloody collision were moved from the actual battle site to burial in neighbouring cemeteries, mostly to the bare and lonely sands of Knightsbridge, this one with an Allied total of 3649, and near Acroma, some 24 kilometres west of Tobruk.

Of the 496 New Zealanders planted forever at Knights-bridge, 435 are in known marked graves. (Those who fought and died but whose graves are unknown are commemorated far to the east on the Alamein Memorial in this dead city, EI Alamein War Cemetery.)

New Zealand dead in three other cemeteries in Libya are Tobruk (38), Benghazi (11) and Tripoli (71). Seventeen kilometres into Egypt 199 New Zealanders are buried at the Halfaya Sollum War Cemetery, where my first Stuka or Messerschmitt, in November 1941, swept with a terrible noise of giants tearing carpets to shreds...

Heeding these things and saving me from bewilerment and inaccuracies, Merv Missen of the Department of Internal Affairs, helped me. Further, he pointed out that 'Intending pilgrims to New Zealand dead from Sidi Rezegh go by car or taxi from Benghazi to Tobruk. An overnight stay at Tobruk is necessary.'

Oh, I do hope that some comrades and countryfolk do more than comfortably grieve over statistics, that some indeed do journey and call for a final goodbye to son, lover, parent, pal...

ESCAPING, bent nearly double, for days a Kiwi POW laboriously carried a great beam of wood to near the Swiss border, where, on the point of grasping freedom, he was nabbed by a vigilant guard and returned to imprisonment vile.

For nigh a broken-hearted week he spoke to nobody, silent and grim, then burst into mad laughter. Had he cracked? Never! 'Could have been worse,' he admitted, heaving with mirth. They could have turned me round and told me to carry the bloody beam all the way back again.'

Beauty! Corker, eh? That's the spirit that saw the war out.

WAY up in Mount Olympus, the sacred mountain, behold, the New Zealanders are having an inspection of teeth, a dental inspection, when wallop! The German comes and they flea in all directions, losing the battle. But behind on Mount Olympus, surely the most extraordinary offering ever to the Gods – two abandoned sacks of artificial teeth and dental plates from the end of the world.

CHAPTER FIVE

At the Pole

THIS is a curious little thing about Captain Scott of the Antarctic. Came in for some criticism because discipline was very strict in those days, particularly in the navy and down in the Antarctic. In Scott's hut, at one stage, they made a little partition of boxes to divide off the officers from lesser ranked sailors. Exactly the same thing happened in the 1950s when Willington Broadcasting house was opened in Bowen Street, Wellington and we moved in — Wheel Talk, Section Head Office, NZBS, as they called it in those days. In these empty new rooms they built up a little barrier of apple cases — we moved all our junk and papers and everything by apple cases in those days. Ken Funnel and our head, Bruce Broadhead, were the two senior officers. There we were, partitioned off exactly as the criticised Captain Scott of the Antarctic and his men had been way back at the beginning of this century.

IN 1960 I was in the Autarctic, on assignment for the New Zealand Broadcasting Service, an experience I later described in *One Foot at the Pole*, published by Whitcombe & Tombs in 1962. The following conversation with an American serviceman, Finn, a Greenpeace advocate before his time, took place outside Scott's Hut, at McMurdo Camp.

'Poor Scott,' says Finn after a bit. 'I'm glad he can't get back. What a shock he'd get. He'd die again.'

'Why, how's that, Finn?'

Finn talks about the chewed up tracks, the casual people coming and going and trooping about 'without *earning* the right to be here', the litter, the empty crates, the trash slung out for the skua gulls to bicker and nag over. The oil streaks in the snow. The roar of motors going twenty-four hours a day. People talking about 'The bus ride, the tram ride'.

'So?'

'Scott wouldn't like that. This Antarctic is a private place. This place is more like a tip.'

'Base camps are always unlovely places. In the Army, anyhow, Finn.'

'Not here too.'

'Look. Scott would get a shock. Of course he would. But he'd get a darned sight worse shock if he returned to nothing. Surely he would? Just empty and silent and still. He and the others were leading up to this.'

'You reckon?'

I suppose from Finn's angle we tourists must be flapping and squawking and picking about like those skua gulls. True enough too. (And the thought of a clean New Zealand 130 years ago, and the blackberry, the gorse, the ragwort, the rabbits coming in...)

'The trouble is people just can't leave things alone. Can't leave people alone, can't leave countries alone.'

'It's wonderful,' I disagree further. 'This to a tourist like me, anyhow this is all that explorer business of shoving on.'

'Maybe this is shoving back.'

'Look, in twenty-five years they'll have a city here. And they'll say what wonderful people you were to come all the way down here with your primitive equipment risking your necks. Your hopeless old fan-driven planes, before anti-gravity ships, before atomic planes even. They'll say those were the pioneers, and people are far too soft in these easy days of the nineties.'

'You think so?'

'I really do, Finn. It's wonderful.'

Finn shakes his head.

ALERT quizmasters! Where, for New Zealanders, is the flag officially raised and lowered only twice in the year? Dawn and dusk? In the Antarctic, of course, of the all-night winter!

Scott Base's historic and venerated flagpole dates back to the one of Scott's Hut of the 1901-04 expedition. Prising it out of ice and snow, the Americans were about to slice into souvenirs, but kndly desisted, agreeing to let Scott Base have it provided, responding to Arthur Helm's and Des Schofield's pleas, it was carried on foot the 2 miles to Scott Base. All okay, and here the New Zealand flag was raised for the first time by Able Seaman R. Tito, a Maori sailor from Waitara.

HOW'S this gentle, pleasing little piece of American-Soviet glasnost learned of, told by James Lennox-King, who took over New Zealand's Antarctic Scott Base as leader in the early pioneer days of 1959? Sven Etveyev was a Soviet liaison officer on duty stationed at the United States Antarctic Base at McMurdo.

His wife was due to produce a baby in Moscow during the long Antarctic winter. Sven confided to James that the winter months would seem doubly long now, with only sparse radio contact then with the rest of the world.

James explains. 'When the baby was born, the Russian Polar Institute arranged for mother and baby to be photographed. They gave the picture to the US Embassy in Moscow, who telegraphed it to Washington, thence to the US Deep Freeze headquarters in Christchurch, who faxed it to McMurdo Base.

'I was invited to the McMurdo gathering where, to his complete surprise and incredulity, Sven was presented with the picture, now framed, of his wife and child less than thirty-six hours after the birth. In an emotional speech Sven dwelt on what, long before, we had all realised: that the Antarctic was not "international", it was "un-national". People of whatever country put aside their national divisions and became, simply, "people of the Antarctic'".

ANOTHER gratifying instance was the Kiwi-Soviet chess contest, Scott versus Mirny, played over hundreds of icy miles in the winter night, the moves, by radio, translated twice at each end by interpreters. The tournament, even for chess, moved with glacier slowness, but amazingly the Kiwis, mostly sketchy at the game, won! The Soviet team included a Grand Master and two Masters, but our inexpert, unconventional and utterly unpredictable play had them completely baffled; to no avail their habitual thinking of twenty moves (even days?) ahead!

One Foot at the Pole
(for Jim)

On a clear morning such as this
he would stand forever,
staring the colourless air
until all in between dissolved
and in his mind's eye
there would be,
as long ago,
the sharp-toothed, cracked antarctic continent
green / flashed with flawless blue,
riding the ice-green sea.
And he grew old,
grew old
bridging the aching distance with a
yearning gaze
until on a day that froze his blood,
the marrow and his very bones
it was so cold,
he turned the rhyme
and through the knife-sharp / glass-exploding
haze,
looked up
and with a sudden and surprising final smile
stood to embrace
his long sought wintertime.

Peggy Dunstan

CHAPTER SIX

Tall Timber

THE Bounce brothers operated their sawmill at the foot of a tremendous kauri, lopping off a limb as orders came. Seven successful years passed. Then an inspector called and disappeared aloft with necessary devices and notebooks. Three days later, he descended.

'It's no good boys,' he told the brothers. 'She's gaining on you.'

A bushman from Finland, indisputably the home of the world's greatest forest workers, applied for a position at New Zealand Forest Products and was asked for his credentials.

'I was a bushfeller in the Sahara.'

'But there are no trees in the Sahara.'

'Correct. Not now.'

ANGRILY, he entered the office of the theatre agent, and slapped down a small box with an oath. 'I detest it. Could be of some interest to you,' he said with a scowl, opening the box, and there, to the astonishment of the agent, at a miniature piano sat a tiny man who at once boldly struck into 'Roses of Picardy'.

'Colossal! A worldwide sensation. Our fortunes are made,' enthused the agent, reaching for agreements and forms in excitement and delight. 'How in the blue blazes did you come to find such a treasure?'

The visitor in annoyance slapped down the lid. The music vanished, to resume again with the little man as active as ever the moment the lid rose.

'The heck with him,' said the chap, 'a bitter disappointment. You see I was going through the woods. A poor old crone tottering with a great bundle of faggots was making her way towards her hovel. I offered to carry the faggots to her doorstep, and throwing the sticks down there, judge my flabbergasted state when in a cloud of light she turned into a beautiful fairy!'

'Kind mortal,' said she, 'for your act, any wish of yours will be instantly granted.'

'Ahrrr!' growled the man, anger renewed, 'just my luck. The old so-and-so must have been deaf. I land up with a nine-inch pianist.'

A rider approaching a bad patch of road (oh yes, definitely a Northland road) then noticed in front of him a man's hat sitting on the mud. He moved forward on foot to retrieve it and was flabbergasted to find it covered a head. He immediately tried to raise the body from beneath, when the head remarked; 'Hang on a minute while I get my feet out of the stirrips.'

IN Otago, a river in furious flood, trees and hen houses swept along in the muddy turmoil, and strolling cautiously by the riverbank, this citizen sees a hat floating along serenely. Judge his amazement when the hat rises a foot, a great red face appears, then submerges, the hat continuing to float along, until again the face rises, gulps, then under again. Amazed, he follows for half a mile.

By now the face has assumed such a violent beetroot colour that the chap becomes thoroughly alarmed. 'I say,' he calls across the torrent, 'can I be of any help?'

'No thanks,' reassures the face, submerging, 'quite all right. I'm on a bicycle.'

STILL in Otago. The wondering tourists admire a clutch of great boulders, and ask where did they come from? The glaciers brought them down, they learn. And where are the glaciers today, they ask?

The guide chirpily replies, 'Why, of course, gone back for more boulders.'

YOUR son, aged seventeen, city weary, strides boldly out, seeking his fortune over our beautiful and surprising countryside. Over a ridge he is amazed to see in the distance a huge woolshed, larger than several city blocks, the sheep-yards stretching nearly to the far horizon, and as he draws nearer, closer in the foreground, a brown lake. Here, two men set out in a dinghy and begin emptying great sacks of some white substance into the lake, then thrash with oars.

'What the dickens you fellers doing in this strange place?' asks the youth, deeply puzzled.

'Preparing morning tea for smokeoh,' comes the reply.

SOUTHLAND the brave, and here gnome-like Arthur Davis tells of the lost Northerner, uncertain of the ways and customs of the Deep South, calling into a wayside pub for further directions, deeply perplexed.

'This old joker I saw was ploughing away, and stopped to give directions by pointing the way *with the plough*. Most unnerving,' said the stranger.

'Oh yeah,' said two teamsters sarcastically, leaning against the bar. 'You'll be saying next time he pointed the horses.'

'What horses?' said the stranger. 'Be blowed! He was pushing the plough.'

DETERMINED to dodge army callup when, in his medical examination, he is asked to read the letters on the card on the wall, he asks blearily, 'What letter, what card, what wall?'

'Hopeless,' they pronounce, dismissing and discharging him.

After a modest lunch, celebrating as a free man again, he drifts into a cinema, sits down to enjoy the film ...and to his unspeakable horror finds himself seated next to the optician who has checked his eyesight. Recovering, in a flash, he inquires: 'Excuse me, but please, am I on the right train for Huntly?'

MAY we now reach for the sky, for heaven, an exceedingly dull day there with much yawning, angels moulting. God approaches St Peter: 'The very thing! A game of golf, Peter.'

Peter gives the Almighty a sceptical glance.

'It's all right,' says God soothingly, 'quite straightforward I assure you.' With a wave of His arm, up springs a superb golf links. God courteously bows to Peter to drive off ... and it's a cracker, to the very lip of the cup.

Happily, God compliments the good saint, who nevertheless appears to be somewhat uneasy, then drives off Himself ...*and it is a real stinker*, hooked away into tiger country, buried in manuka to the end of the cliff.

And an earthquake peels off the edge of the cliff, the ball falls into the sea where a snapper swallows it, the waterspout hurls this fish far into the sky where a fishing eagle flying over snaps up the fish which is shattered to fragments by a bolt of lightning which in turn sends the ball scooting down to the fairway, to the green, and behold ...incredible, but to (and into!) the very cup itself. Hole in one!

A satisfied and well-done-indeed look passes over God's face. The saint steadily regards the Higher Authority, and gathers himself and his wits together.

'With every respect, Sire, before we go further, may we get something straight? Are we playing golf ...or silly buggers?'

CHAPTER SEVEN

Amps

INTO the Christchurch limb factory strode an amputee with what looked like a bundle of fish and chips under his arm, and a twisted clump of mangled manuka roots stuck where his artificial foot should have been. As he unwrapped his foot from the bundle, the limb–fitters, justifiably taken aback, asked, reasonably enough, 'What the hell have you been up to?'

Their client, a solo fisherman, explained that his little boat had suddenly sunk in a freak violent storm off Kaikoura. He'd managed to swim ashore, but during several miles of rugged stomping along the boulders of the coast seeking aid, his foot had come off.

'Never come at that again!' counselled the good considerate limb-fitters, agog. 'Get rid of the thing next time. Kick off the heavy leg to swim ashore, eh?'

'you're stupider than you look,' answered our hero. 'How the blazes would I walk along the beach for help, then?'

SHOCKINGLY wounded at Cassino, amputee Bruce Martin, determined despite warnings not to ride a fiery horse, mounted, clanking and glinting, to be met with the most voluminous sigh he has ever heard. The horse, so evidently showing compassion, moved off at a snail's pace.

WITH both of his legs lost at Cassino, disobeying instructions in a minefield, General Kippenberger is reputed to have promptly asked his wife did she want him, taller, shorter, or as before?

SALVATION Army padre amp Sam Hayes of Fort Dorset, Wellington, forever happy and smiling, was changing a tyre when the jack slipped, the wheel trapping him by his outspread false leg.

An eventual helper arriving wondered greatly:'What manner of man was this to smilingly welcome me while pinned to the ground by an obviously badly crushed leg?'

WHEN he came around after his amputation, we saw the Maori soldier working his remaining leg up and down, up and down, under the blanket. Someone moved towards him, one of the orderlies, and the soldier said, 'My old leg, he's gone?'

'Yes, mate,' said the attendant. 'It was the best thing to do. You'll be alright.'

He thought for a moment and then a smile of happiness crossed over his face, and he said, 'Home, home by Christmas!'

AN atrocious leg splattered with stale blood and manure hove into the disgusted limb factory, Wellington.

'The hell with that!' cried the fitters, affronted, then relenting, hosing and scrubbing it down with a bass broom and much disinfectant in the courtyard. 'Never again,' they wrote firmly in a note to the remote sheepfarmer, posting it back to him.

An almost tearfully apologetic letter replied. When he drove away hastily for a few days in Auckland, he'd called briefly to his wife to post his spare leg down to Wellington for a quick checkover. This spare he kept in a cupboard.

'What possessed her I'll never know,' wrote the chap. 'She went to the sheepyards and bunged off the wrong leg, a frightful old peg leg I keep under a sack and hunk of corrugated iron by the yards and wear only for yarding and marking sheep.'

FOR five and a half weeks Philippa Shields, an attractive twenty-two-month-old child lay unconscious, the victim of a severe accident, leaving her with most severe multiple injuries, including head injuries, with balancing and moving difficulties to master, and a most badly damaged leg, with nerves to the other almost totally severed.

If her beloved daughter did live would she have a mind? And the awful thought — if utterly deprived — would you want her to live?

The long, nearly impossible struggle for recovery began and, learning of Philippa's eventual triumph and epic crossing of the Heaphy Track (where I myself had failed, the upper leather part of my artificial leg, lucklessly, becoming soaked overnight and turning it into a mincer), I urged emphatically for an account − parly to complete the trip, like this, in my mind too.

Philippa's mother, cabinet minister, Margaret Shields, an attractive, couth and immensely capable woman, gave me this story which I treasure.

It all had been a terrible blow but somehow the fact that Philippa's mind was still there got the whole problem into perspective − at least for us. The rest of the world was more difficult to deal with. For the next ten years, until Philippa's leg was finally amputated, we concentrated on encouraging her to do anything she wanted to do, while other people kept on behaving as if the only important thing about her was that she was 'crippled'. While we encouraged her to do as much as she could, by − at times − literally sitting on our hands while she picked herself up, others regarded us as unbelievably hardhearted.

The local Crippled Children's field officer wasn't always a great help. She was constantly telling me that Philippa's boots were wearing out too quickly, or her calipers were breaking because I was letting her do unsuitable things. Tough! It was worth it. Philippa's mind and spirit had to be more important than her leg.

By the time Philippa was in her teens she was prepared to have a go at most things, but when she decided to walk the Heaphy Track even I was doubtful. We knew the track and the idea of doing it on crutches filled us with trepidation. The track is 78 kilometres long and has six accommodation huts.

I told her we'd have to train for that exercise. I wasn't

prepared to take her on such a jaunt unless she could prove she could manage. Philippa was not daunted. She started with a climb to the top of Johnstons Hill in Karori – a piece of cake! Then we went up to the top of Kapiti Island – a bit tricky but the terrain is much worse than anything you might find on the Heaphy. We followed that with a week-end visit to the Orongorongo Valley. No real problems, so I agreed.

Philippa's father couldn't come so I arranged to take a couple of young fellows with us. We contacted the Forest Service and planning began.

Tramping on crutches wasn't my biggest concern. One of the tasks worrying me was 'How do you go over wire-netting swing bridges?' Philippa found a way – she just practised hopping over them and the swing bridges which had always horrified me now proved no difficulty.

But the sheer physical effort required was almost too much. We got a lot of help from the Forest Service. We left from the Bainham and the Forest Service helped us up the first but to within a mile of the Perry Saddle Hut. So, kindly, we were there by lunch and went on to the Gouland Downs Hut, still escorted by the Forest Service – a great comfort to me as my greatest fear was the Cave Brook Bridge, a suspension bridge spanning a narrow canyon and approached from each sided by a sheer rock face. Philippa managed like a trouper, not knowing the vivid nightmare I'd had the night before of her falling off the Cave Brook Bridge.

The next day was much more difficult. The Gouland Downs is tussock country, the track narrow and very difficult on crutches. Our first problem was Philippa losing a crutch stopper in a bog; they were arm–crutches of metal. We whittled a new stopper out of beech wood. The second problem was more insidious.

Philippa started to get more clumsy — the first sign of exposure. I started to get worried. We were still a long way from the next hut. Suddenly round the corner came a Forest Service fellow on a pony — the Lone Ranger couldn't have been more helpful or more welcome.

He got off and she got on; she had learned to ride with Riding for the Disabled. But the saddle kept slipping because of Philippa having only the one leg; she usually rode sidesaddle. No problem — the guy had a couple of sacks and we put a few rocks in and balanced her up. To cut a long story short, we made it through the track, not without difficulty — blistered hands, falls down banks, exhaustion — but we made it.

Philippa will probably never take on anything as physically challenging again, but she has never regretted doing it. She is now married and the mother of a couple of small children. What was the point? The main point, really, is that Philippa sees herself as someone who can cope, will have a go and knows her limits. She ought to, she has touched the edge of them.

She never asks for favours. She understands other people very well. She could have become a queralous, demanding person. She hasn't. She knows how to ask or help when she really needs it. Otherwise she just gets on with it.

That's what most disabled people want — the opportunity to get on with it without being smothered by the self-serving overconcern of others.

FIRST come to a lake in Canada. I would remove my left leg, swim, hop back to resume the limb, and behold! Gathered like cattle before the water trough, interested but good-intentioned Canadians, who would recall aunts or other relatives who, after enduring endless amputations and setbacks, finally expired. Inside, I would wince, while outside I would grin weakly and say, 'Sure, sure yeah.'

But in the land of the English, at Penzance, before breakfast, I was hopping down the beach to the breakers, when an old gruff colonel-type Englishman marched past me, with just a curt 'Morning' tossed over his shoulder.

At that moment I stubbed my toe on a rock and sat down, cursing. Not a word did he say about afflicted aunts or anything else. No sir! Straight on into the waves he strode, not looking back, but calling firmly, 'Dammit man, can't you walk on your hands?'

I'd have followed him into a volcano.

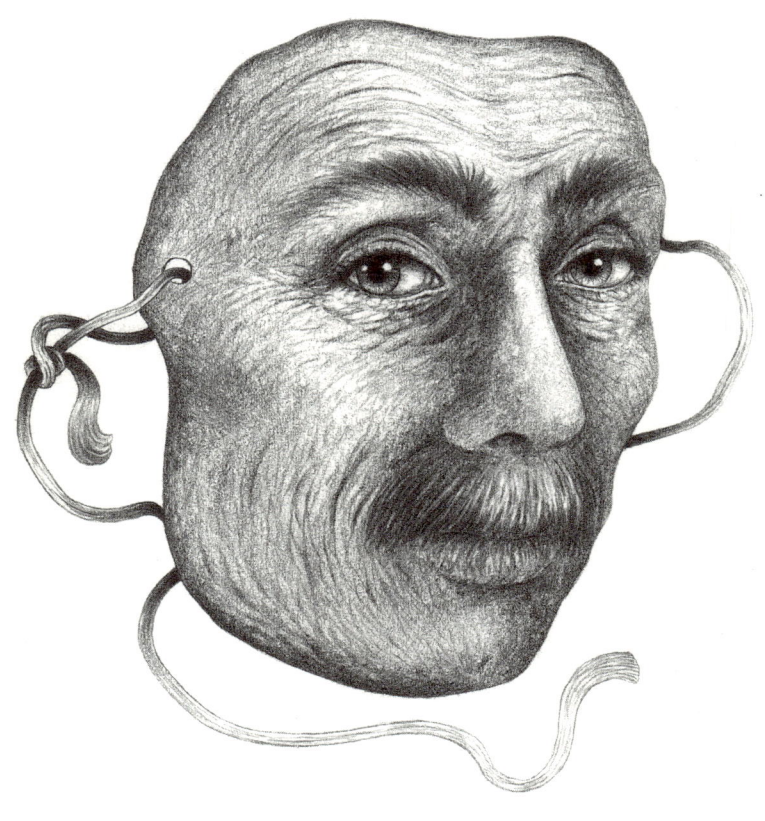

CHAPTER EIGHT

Surprise Surprise

WHEN Doctor Gray author of *The Very Edge of the Moon*, was head of the mental hospital in Nelson, he keenly advocated concerts given by the patients at the mental Hospital. He invited a timid and hesitant friend from far parts to come along to a concert, which passed off superbly. The apprehensive visitor sat next to the doctor on the stage, for reassurance.

Chatting to Doctor Gray afterwards he said, 'A very good concert. Looking over the audience they all appeared to be pretty nearly normal, pleasant people. But, by jove, I didn't like the look of that row of people near the very front row. They made me nervy.

Doctor Gray laughed.

'Why?' said the visitor.

'Old chap, that was the hospital board.'

WHILE we're on this subject, the old sergeant major, as predicted, was confined to a mental hospital and came out in a state of great excitement, several years later.

'My superb discovery!' he said. 'Sensational!'

They took the dear old man down to his cell and 'Behold,' he said, producing a matchbox and a beetle. On the table he placed the beetle. 'Now watch.' He roared at the beetle, 'Attention!' The beetle sprang to attention. 'Right turn!Quick march!' Smartly to the right; then off it went. 'Left wheel!' And it wheeled to the left. 'Beetle, halt.' It did. 'Stand at ease, stand easy.'

'Amazing,' applauded the superintendent. 'This display really will create a stir around the world.'

'Ha ha! One moment, please,' said the old sergeant major. 'Noting compared to what it will do now!' And with that he produced a pair of plastic scissors which are permitted in certain institutions. And he snipped off the beetle's legs, then put the poor remnant down on the table and shouted: 'Beetle, attention! Move to the left. Left turn, quick march. Halt. Right turn. Stand at ease. Stand easy.'

Not a fraction from the beetle, now completely motionless. The old sergeant major turned to the superintendent.

'There!' said he in triumph. 'My great discovery! I've proved conclusively that a beetle hears through its legs.'

A very sophisticated party in Paris, a chap who is connected with the New Zealand diplomatic corps told me, and a most attractive girl, of Yugoslav origin, came up to him said, 'We are leaving for New Zealand shortly. What a magnificent country it must be.'

He said, 'Why choose New Zealand?'

She said, 'There was a little village in Yugoslavia when I was only a little girl and it was a Sunday morning. The Germans, who had recently occupied our country, where having the morning off. They were gathered in this little village and some were close to the bridge. one was actually sitting on the edge of the bridge, on the railing and they were all cleaning their boots, their shoes, everything, even their buckles were glistening. Even the Germans' teeth were flashing in the sun.'

At that stage along came a ragged depressed bunch of Kiwis slouching along under guard. They looked a desperate crowd. They'd just been captured and you couldn't blame

them. However, the Germans as good soldiers do, just did not mock or make rude gestures at the prisoners going past. You just didn't look. The Germans continued with their polishing, their flashing and the ragged Kiwis came slouching along, over the bridge, except for the last Kiwi coming along. As he passed the German who was sittting on the edge of the bridge polishing away at his buckle, the Kiwi turned to the left and raised his right hand with a finger pointing, close to the Grman and went 't-t-t-t-t-t-t-t-t-t-t', as if shooting up the German, who got such a shock, head over tip into the river he went.

The Yugoslav woman relating this said, 'Well, they could have erased the village if they had wanted to. All the atrocities and things that could have happened. We didn't give a darn. The memory of that Kiwi going "t-t-t-t" and the German flat over somersault into the river gave us the courage, the humour and the inspiration to see the wretched war out in Yugoslavia and that is why I thought the people who are produced like that, come from New Zealand, that will be good enough for us.'

AN English tourist rose early on the magnificent West Coast, went out of his little country hotel, strolled down the garden path and made use of the little house down the bottom of the path. Coming back furiously to the host, he said, livid, 'in all my travels round the world... I came down early this morning, down to the little house down the back and it was full of bluebottles. The air was thick with these flies. Disgraceful! never before have I seen such a shocking sight. Surely you can rectify it!'

'Certainly,' said the Coaster publican, beaming. 'Do what we all do. Go down there for your visit when it's breakfast time. They're all in the kitchen then.'

JOCK Matheson, politician of Christchurch, with a splendid Scottish background and sense of humour, was telling me all about Walter Nash addressing them in Parliament. He was talking about the guaranteed price, tossing endless figures in millions and fractions into the electrified air.

'This,' he told the House, 'brings the figure to £149,743,200 and tenpence,' and so forth and so on. They were spellbound and absolutely staggered by the deft bombardment of it all.

'And finally,', as the great climax, we heard, never to forget, Walter Nash, this wizard of finance, come to the following stupendous conclusion: 'We have set up a committee of twelve to look into it. Eight of them and two of us.'

CHAPTER NINE

Dogs

'YOU'RE still a pup at heart, it's just the zest of you that's got old,' Derek Ward, in the yards drenching hoggets and lambs, Feilding, July ...you get this in the yards, not in library research.

SANDY, a mature Labrador, say aged seven, always embarrassed my mother, no one else: he'd find the most maggoty old pukeko run over on the road, and tenderly drop it at her feet, preferably when she was greeting or farewelling posh guests. If all else failed, his last resort, all doleful-eyed, was to break wind with the most appalling smell imaginable.

He (a magnificent game dog to give him his due) excelled himself when Rosy the house cow died.

'Cut off her legs so we don't have to bury her so deep,' we said.

'Is nothing sacred? Dig deeper,' replied Dad.

They have a sense of humour, animals do — can sense when there is tension or undue animation in the house. Several weeks went by. Sandy began coming home with a muddy nose. 'After rabbits,' Mrs Ward senior would say.

An instinctive, true artist, Sandy was biding his time; he had a sense of occasion. So to our most elegant of Mum's morning tea parties, her absolute pinnacle of hen parties, and up the drive comes Sandy.

'What's your dog carrying?' Gracious speculation and polite cooing galore...

Right to Mum's feet he brings his ghastly contribution to ruin festivities and appetites: he'd removed and was carrying by one semi-elastic teat, the entire udder from the dear decayed Rosy.

A dog called King, a terrific heading dog. Nearby, a 90-acre dairy farmer about 80 cents in the $1, always shouting when he visited, so that King, with increasing ferocity and resentment, would snarl and tooth at this, a habit which developing into racing out and gnawing the front tyre of the shouting caller's truck.

The next step was to try and grab him through the window if possible. One day, foiled by the half-raised window, king took a flying leap at Old F____, who later appeared with a muzzle, saying, 'Use this or I'll have him destroyed by the police.'

Muzzle King? never! So, sadly he was sold to George up the way, at Hunterville.

Time passes. They meet.

'How's King going, George?'

'He's starting to go good on stock. I'll never pass with him.'

'Developed as good as that, eh?'

'Well, er, sort of. That gardener I've got is half dopey. King just stands a few yards off and snarls at him. He used to do the rose garden in one and a half days. He does it in four hours now.'

THIS next tale tells a wee bit more about men than perhaps is intended to.

Three old cockies were sitting on the verandah boasting and skiting about their dogs.

'Course my dog,' said one, 'is the champion. Just watch. Go out,' said he to his dog lying at the foot of the verandah. 'Go out and bring in the black and white calf.' And off went the dog and sure enough out of a whole lot of varied coloured calves back came the black and white one requested. Excellent job.

'I'll knock that easily,' said the old cocky. 'Jack! On your way, Jack, and bring back a ram and an old ewe.' Away he went and sure enough after a while back came the dog who'd cut out a ram and an old, old ewe — very decrepit.

'Splendid,' said the second farmer.

The third said, 'Ha, ha. That's what you think. Just watch. He's the champion without the slightest doubt. Top!

Top off you go and round up the three biggest rams in the district.

And away went Top, this beloved dog. At least an hour passed and they were going to pack it in and say, 'Oh well, poor ole Top, yeah, he'd failed miserably', when suddenly a great commotion over the horizon and then a cloud of dust and then shouting and angry voices. But remorselessly, up to the verandah, driven by the brilliant dog Top, came the schoolteacher, the blacksmith and the parson.

SHANE was a bearded jet black huntaway with that look of incipient mischievousness beardies specialise in. Shane could back cattle as well. When Alex Ward suggested he could load the fourteen dairy cows, which for some two hours, despite every inducement and violence, had defied the now demented farmer, he met with the scornful reply: 'All we want − a sheep cocky's mongrel to end everything.'

The truck driver, also fed up, was about to leave. 'I've wasted enough time as it is.'

Alex repeated his offer, despite the dairy farmer's disbelief and scorn, inviting the driver to quit the cab and open all the gates in the crate and stand clear. The driver, sceptial, chose to stay in the crate and clear. The driver, sceptical, chose to stay in the crate, reckoning they'd maybe drift by, in ones and twos. . .

Shane landed fair bang on the back of the boss cow and barked in her ear, a novelty in bovine circles. She bounded aboard, and en masse the remaining thirteen cows, similarly encouraged, rose straight into the crate, shaking it violently, with muffled shouts from the besieged driver.

Then, the dust settling, fearful the dog might be trampled, the cry arose: 'Where's Shane?'

They found the noble dog had made his escape un-

scathed. Furthermore, thinking, 'Here's a bit of fair go',
Shane now, for good measure, was busily mating with the
farmer's bitch, a few yards away under the macrocarpa
tree.

'Our dog's had a good day,' was the summary.

THE local dealers, whose transactions in dogs and horses were shuffled through with the dexterity of playing cards, was having a spot of bother suiting his latest seeker of a canine work mate. Finally, after a hat-tilting head scratch, his eye fell on an old upturned tank. Purposefully he strode towards it, his distinctive voice booming: 'I've got another good dog over here.' He raised the tank to a stunned silence, for there lay one very thoroughly dead dog. Came the awed comment: 'That's funny! he's never done that before − I only fed him last night!'

CAN a sheepdog be too obedient? They say on Lake Wakatipu, while sheep were being loaded onto the *Earnslaw*, an old ewe sprang overboard, the boss sent his too−obedient sheepdog swimming after her. He brought her round okay and just seemed to be crowding her slightly, so the boss yelled out: 'Sit down!'

The obedient dog did so − and hasn't been seen since.

'DANCING the Pommy Waltz' − that's what Kiwis call it, dodging dog manure on the payments in London.

TUSSOCK country in the land of the brave, but alas the tussock stood too high on this hillside where the faithful huntaway, really tearing away at top speed, a bark at every step, struck a partly concealed iron standard, and tragically was split in half, nose to tail!

Resourceful shepherds instantly sewed up old Toss, but alas, a bit careless through concern, stitched one half the wrong way up!

All was by no means lost. Mastering the art of running on two legs, the noble animal, when tiring, only had to be reversed, turned over and, in a flash, behold, good as a fresh dog again!

THE old Cocky, like others getting on, really was too blind to lend a hand', as he irritatingly put it, with mustering. This time, calling across the valley, mistaking a small white stump for a straggler, he was working his loyal but utterly mystified dog back and forth and even over the stump.

The head shepherd had stood enough foolery up the valley: 'Try fitting a blade on him, you silly old bugger, and you might do better!'

FAIR go! Even the gnarled old sheepdogs shut their eyes, and *wince*, I have seen them, Scout's honour, when old Dave ('Kairuria') Henderson has them chained to the back of the battered farmtruck or Land Rover, and raving along the tapeworm thin trail of boulders and slips, teetering along the very edge of his percipices bordering the Round Hill and the foaming river below. Great love, indeed, hath the sheepdog ...

CRINGING in the furthermost corner of the kennel, hiding in sheds, or slinking up house steps in search of an open door and sanctuary beneath a bed, is not uncommon among dogs of all breeds and sizes when thunder and lightning do battle.

But Blue, of high IQ and ability, erupted into frantic and distinctive activity. Dashing out from his kennel he would, while uttering protesting yelps, dig furiously at the earth in front of his kenel. (Had he at sometime been a prairie dog, or maybe a slittie-digging soldier in the desert?)

The length of the storm determined the number of holes he dug, the depth up to about eight inches, and he would never resist, even when the overworked paws were bleeding, which often happened through successive stormy weather. Of course the deluge of rain would fill the holes and it was an unforgettable sight to see his kennel balance on a patch of ground and surrounded by what appeared to be almost a moat, over which he must hop to gain entrance once calm was restored.

The Companion Volume

A collection of funny and often very moving stories about Kiwis past and present. Tributes to what Jim calls the 'heroic everyday' people.

Available from 'Booksellers' and other good bookstores